ISIL's Reign of Terror: Confronting the Growing Humanitarian Crisis in Iraq and Syria

Senate Foreign Relations Committee

December 9, 2014

Table of Contents

Testimony

Department of State, Bureau of Democracy,

Human Rights, and Labor

Written Testimony for Assistant Secretary Tom Malinowski

Senate Foreign Relations Committee hearing on "ISIL's Reign

of Terror: Confronting the Growing Humanitarian

Crisis in Iraq and Syria"

Tuesday, December 9, 2014, 10:00am

Subcommittee on International Operations and Organizations,

Human Rights, Democracy, and Global Women's Issues

Chairwoman Boxer and Members of the Committee, thank you for holding this important and timely hearing on the Islamic State of Iraq and the Levant's (ISIL) egregious human rights abuses in Iraq and Syria. We are meeting at a time when our ideals and interests are being tested in many places, but perhaps most starkly in the rise of the so called Islamic State, or Daesh. Not for the first time, we're seeing that our ability to imagine evil rarely measures up to the reality of mass executions, ethnic cleansing, the enslavement of women, and the murder of innocent Americans who came to the Middle East for the sole purpose of helping people and telling the world about their fate. The toll on a region already under stress has been extraordinary—over 1.5 million Iraqis have been displaced, while in Syria, civilians pressed from one side by Asad's barrel bombs and starvation sieges are now pressed from the other by this vicious terror group. Throughout the region, Daesh has destroyed hundreds of mosques and shrines, demolished Christian icons and crosses, and taken sledgehammers to the tombs of saints revered in Islam, Judaism and Christianity.

As enemies of human rights go, Daesh is in a unique class. Not because it uses bombings, assassinations or kidnappings to terrorize people, but because it targets entire ethnic and religious groups for particularly horrific and persistent violence, simply because of whom they are. It murders men who won't agree to accept its warped ideology. It seizes women not only as hostages but as commodities, spoils of war to be raped or sold. There are tyrants in the world who commit such crimes, but they know on some level that their conduct is shameful, so they hide what they do; Daesh puts its crimes on YouTube. It is of the utmost importance that those who commit and brag about such acts not be allowed to project a narrative of success, as Daesh tried to do earlier this year. It must fail and be seen to fail by every person and organization around the world that might have similar inclinations.

And Daesh will fail; there is no question about that now. By targeting people of all sects, religions, and nationalities, it has united people of all sects, religions, and nationalities against it, and enabled us to forge a global coalition in support of local forces that will ultimately defeat this organization and liberate people from its terror. We will restore human rights by defeating Daesh. But what I want to stress most of all today is that the reverse is also true: we will defeat Daesh in part by defending the human rights of its intended victims. The protection of civilians in

Iraq and Syria is built into our strategy; we see it not just as a moral imperative but a key to success in the fight.

We know we can't defeat Daesh through airpower alone; we can do so only in partnership with allies on the ground, including members of local communities in the areas where Daesh operates, from Sunni tribes in Iraq and Syria, to Kurds in both countries, to groups like the Yezidis. Members of these communities will want to partner with us if we continue to show them that this campaign is aimed at protecting them, and they will be able to partner with us if we help in the effort to bring them some relief from terror attacks. Moreover, Daesh benefits from atrocities committed by others. It arose in part because a dictator in Syria has spent the last three years destroying towns and cities, driving half the people of his country from their homes, until some of them became so desperate that they turned to the false deliverance Daesh offered. It ascended in part because many Iraqi Sunnis felt their legitimate grievances were ignored, or created, by the previous government in Baghdad. A campaign of prison breaks, the execution of former *Sahwa* leaders and moderate Sunnis, and virtually no protection from the central government left some Iraqi Sunnis at the mercy of Daesh's tactics.

By demonstrating concern for the welfare and protection of civilians in Iraq and Syria, we gain allies on the ground and build the foundations of resilient, rights-respecting societies in which extremist groups will have fewer grievances to prey on. Let me describe more specifically what we are doing:

First, we are protecting the most vulnerable people from Daesh's reach. To that end, the United States has developed and led a coalition of 60 international partners, to include leaders in the Islamic world, in a campaign to defeat, degrade, and delegitimize Daesh and its campaign of horrors.

Working with our coalition partners, we have come to the aid of members of communities targeted by Daesh on several occasions and dealt it strategic blows, halting its advance and preventing further atrocities. In August, as Daesh began its attack on the Yezidis on Mt. Sinjar, President Obama ordered airstrikes to avert a potential act of genocide and to protect American personnel in Iraq. The United States delivered114,000 meals and 35,000 gallons of water via air drops during the first week alone. The airstrikes helped many Yezidis flee Mt. Sinjar for safety. As the crisis on Sinjar unfolded, my staff was in continuous contact with Yezidis in Iraq and the diaspora, including those still on Mt. Sinjar and women and girls held captive by Daesh. In September, our airstrikes broke Daesh's two-month siege of the Iraqi town of Amerli, where an estimated 15,000 Turkmen Shia were surrounded. Over the past two months, our airstrikes in Kobani--also called Ayn al-Arab--have helped to break another siege and allowed Kurdish and other fighters to push back Daesh militants' gains in northern Syria.

In the bureau I lead, we actively seek information from our contacts about vulnerable civilian populations still in harm's way, including female captives, and the movements of Daesh forces threatening them. We are working closely with CENTCOM, sharing this information in real time, so that they can act on the information when appropriate. And we have seen results where coalition action, coordinated with Iraqi ground operations, has directly supported members of vulnerable civilian populations and their needs, including protecting Yezidis remaining near Mt. Sinjar, and, given its importance to civilians, taking back the Mosul Dam. As more Iraqis, especially Sunnis, in Daesh-controlled areas rule rise up against them, we will be very attentive to the extra risk to them and their families stemming from that decision. In late October and early November in Anbar Province, Daesh executed over 300 members of the Albu Nimr tribe, including women and children, after the tribe decided to side with Iraqi forces against Daesh. Other members of the tribe had been able to flee. On October 27, we air dropped food to Iraqi forces to provide to members of the Albu Nimr tribe who had recently fled from their homes to Al Asad Air Base to avoid retaliation.

When Iraqi forces, including Kurdish forces, liberate territory captured by Daesh, they will need to be alert to the possibility of last minute reprisal attacks against vulnerable civilians, and captives to the needs of the people who suffered most, including any hostages who may be able to escape or be rescued. We are taking all these challenges into account in planning future efforts.

Second, we are strengthening civil society and governance structures on the ground.

In Iraq, we are supporting Prime Minister Abadi's efforts to reach across sectarian lines and to demonstrate inclusivity. We have urged the Iraqi Government to further Prime Minister Abadi's proposed reforms to reduce sectarian divisions, to strengthen inclusivity in its security sector, and to promote reconciliation in Iraq. The test of the Abadi government starts now, in the conduct of the campaign against Daesh, which must persuade all Iraq's communities—from Shia who are constant targets of Daesh attacks, to minorities, to Sunnis who have felt disenfranchised by the Iraqi government and threatened by Shia militias—that they will be welcome and secure in Iraq under a non-sectarian government and a security sector to protect it. One possible mechanism for incorporating Christians, Yezidis, and Sunnis into the security infrastructure is through the new National Guard. Such an action may help provide these communities with representation and a role in their own protection—something they have long sought. Prime Minister Abadi took an important step December 2 by issuing an Executive Order to address some of the grievances of the Sunnis and uphold the rule of law. It would enforce legal limits on detentions of those who have not yet been charged and to expedite the release of those detainees who have been ordered to be freed by the courts. Abadi has shown he wishes to govern in a manner different than that of his predecessors and highlighted a "zero tolerance" policy for human rights abuses.

We do not have to pursue this endeavor alone. We will work in tandem with our over 60 coalition partners, including the Government of Iraq, to address atrocity prevention, stabilization, and recovery in a post-Daesh

Iraq and Syria, and hold Daesh accountable for its actions. Secretary Kerry and General John Allen further elaborated these strategies at the December 3 Ministerial in Brussels.

In Syria, we face even greater challenges, and we are obviously not yet where we need to be. The vast majority of Syrians want to rid their country of Daesh, but the communities most threatened are caught in a vise between the terrorists and the Asad regime. In February and July, we supported UN Security Council resolutions on Syria that sought to force the Asad regime to end atrocities and permit entry of humanitarian assistance, and we remain committed to a political solution that will stop the killing and lead to an inclusive government. But the regime continues to defy all efforts to resolve the crisis.

Coalition airstrikes have helped to arrest the progress of Daesh in northern and eastern Syria, providing some relief and buying some time for the armed moderate opposition and civilians to regain their strength. Our planned support for the armed moderate opposition will help them do more to protect their people in liberated areas and to push back the terrorists. Amidst all the bad news from Syria, it is important to remember that there is a great deal in these liberated areas that is worth defending and that can be built upon to achieve a better future for Syria. Dedicated Syrians are bravely trying to maintain local self-government, police and judicial institutions, to keep open schools, to deliver services, to rescue people hurt by fighting, and to rebuild what is constantly being destroyed. I sometimes fear that when people think about Syria, they imagine a place populated by nothing more than terrorists and Asad loyalists, with no one in between who can partner with us and inspire any hope. That is a cruel and dangerous falsehood.

We have provided $330 million in non-lethal support to the Syrian Opposition Coalition (SOC), local opposition councils, and civil society groups, to help Syria's moderate center stay alive. U.S. assistance is also being directed to maintain public safety and to mitigate sectarian violence. Assistance includes training and equipment to build the capacity of a network of more than 3,000 grassroots activists from more than 400 opposition councils and organizations from around the country. This assistance program links Syrian citizens with the national and local-level Syrian opposition. It also enhances linkages among Syrian activists, human rights organizations, and independent media outlets and empowers women leaders to play a more active role in transition planning.

After Daesh is defeated, effective governance will be critical to establishing and maintaining stability. Reintegration of displaced persons, recovery of basic services, and security will be essential to put affected areas on the road to stabilization. In Iraq, we will support this government's efforts to govern inclusively and to take significant, concrete steps to address the legitimate grievances and needs of all Iraqis. In Syria, we will continue to support efforts to pursue a political solution that will result in a united, inclusive, and democratic Syria.

Third, we are specifically seeking to support women and children.

The U.S. Government provides psychological, medical, and social support, as well as case management and legal assistance, to Syrian women and children inside Syria and in refugee-hosting countries throughout the region. This support is delivered through reproductive health care efforts, the creation of women-friendly spaces, mobile clinics, and outreach workers. Through the *Gender-Based Violence Emergency Response and Protection Initiative*, we have provided emergency assistance to survivors of extreme forms of gender-based violence and harmful traditional practices. This has included the provision of emergency medical and psychosocial support to dozens of Yezidi women and girls formerly held captive by Daesh, who suffered the most egregious forms of sexual and gender-based violence.

We see a connection between protection of women and their participation in civil life and governance. U.S. support inside Syria is empowering women and girls to take an active role in governance and civic engagement, and we are working to amplify the voices of Syrian women civil society leaders participating in peacebuilding initiatives. In Iraq, we are providing training for tens of thousands of Iraqi students on rights awareness, violence prevention, and advocacy initiatives to promote legislation on gender equality. In addition, the U.S. Government supports campaigns to educate on the dangers of early and forced marriage across the region.

Fourth, officials throughout the Administration are working closely with representatives of religious communities and other vulnerable groups in Iraq and Syria.

These contacts share information about Daesh's abuses and humanitarian conditions facing members of displaced communities. Our Embassies, various bureaus in the State Department (including my own), and other U.S. agencies have extensive contacts with religious leaders like the Patriarch of the Syriac Catholic Church, advocacy and aid groups like International Christian Concern and Catholic Relief Services, and human rights organizations like Yezidi Human Rights Organization-International.

In October, we brought a Syrian religious delegation to the United States to discuss interfaith issues. One participant, the well-known Sunni Sheikh Mohammed Yaqoubi, formerly the Imam of the Grand Umayyad Mosque in Damascus, engaged U.S. media—including CNN and PBS—and Muslim American communities across the United States to condemn Daesh and discourage American Muslims from joining Daesh and other extremist groups. He also led a Friday Muslim funerary prayer for Peter Kassig in his Indiana hometown, in the presence of Kassig's mother and father, where he spoke against Daesh in the strongest possible terms. His lectures of moderation and tolerance in Los Angeles, Chicago, and New York drew thousands.

Throughout the Administration, both in Washington and in the region, we are collaborating with religious leaders and communities to address the underlying causes of and motivations for violent extremism, religious intolerance, and societal polarization. We are working with NGOs, civil society groups, and religious leaders to build relationships between religious communities, to combat terrorist propaganda about religious minorities, and to administer programs that promote tolerance and empower minorities to better advocate for their interests and rights. We are helping to strengthen grassroots organizations and local administrative bodies—foundations of democratic governance—as they step in to fill the void left by the Syrian regime and to provide basic services.

Fifth, we are supporting documentation of atrocities to hold all actors accountable.

Accountability is important. To establish a peaceful, inclusive political solution in Syria and effective, inclusive governance in Iraq that undermines and ultimately defeats Daesh, we must remain committed to seeking justice for victims of atrocities and accountability for those responsible for such heinous crimes; there can only be lasting peace if there is justice.

We have supported the work of the UN Independent International Commission of Inquiry, which recently released a report entitled, "*Rule of Terror: Living under ISIS in Syria*." This report gathered information from more than 300 courageous Syrian men, women, and children, who shared accounts of Daesh's cruelty and inhumane treatment, including mass executions, sexual violence against women and girls, ethnic cleansing, recruitment of child soldiers, forced displacement, and targeting of journalists. The U.S. Government co-sponsored the UN Human Rights Council resolution requesting the UN Office of the High Commissioner for Human Rights dispatch a mission to Iraq to investigate alleged violations and abuses of international human rights law by ISIL and associated terrorist groups. The Office is documenting Daesh's abuses committed in Iraq and will improve the ability of local authorities to promote and protect the human rights of affected communities.

The Department of State has programs to enable Iraqi and Syrian civil society to document human rights abuses to serve a wide range of future transitional justice purposes, including, but not limited to truth-telling, reconciliation, reparations, institutional reform, memorialization, evidence collection, and criminal accountability. We are supporting a number of initiatives focused on transitional justice and atrocity documentation, aimed at bolstering accountability for atrocities committed by all sides. The United States, along with eight other governments, supports the Syria Justice and Accountability Center (SJAC) as one of the premier Syrian-led institutions leading this documentation effort through its database, analysis, training, and networks inside Syria. The information collected lays the groundwork for future accountability processes, including potential criminal prosecutions.

We are also committed to promoting justice and accountability for those responsible for Daesh's atrocities in Iraq by working with the Iraqi

Government, other partners in the region, and the international community in supporting domestic justice and accountability efforts.

Chairwoman Boxer, members of the Committee, as you know this fight will not be won easily or quickly. But the protection of human rights is not merely the endpoint of the fight; it is the starting point; it is the way we will win.

This is not just a campaign against a group of people; it is a campaign for human dignity and justice, for the right of all to live in safety. Each time we succeed in protecting someone from Daesh, whether we are working with an entire religious community, like the Yezidis or the Christians, a single village, or a single person, we gain a strategic victory for ourselves and strike a moral and psychological blow to Daesh.

**Testimony of the U.S. Agency for International Development
Assistant Administrator Nancy Lindborg before the
Senate Foreign Relations Subcommittee on International
Operations and Organizations, Human Rights, Democracy, and
Global Women's Issues
Hearing entitled "ISIL's Reign of Terror: Confronting the
Growing Humanitarian Crisis in Iraq and Syria"
December 9, 2014**

Introduction

Chairwoman Boxer, Ranking Member Paul and Members of the Subcommittee, thank you for the opportunity to testify today on the humanitarian crisis in Syria and Iraq. Many thanks to the Subcommittee for holding this important hearing and shining a light on the devastating humanitarian situation and abhorrent human rights abuses committed by the terrorist organization known as the Islamic State of Iraq and the Levant (ISIL), which as President Obama rightly clarified, is neither Islamic nor a State.

The Syrian crisis is the largest and most complex humanitarian emergency of our time, and it has now mutated into a regional humanitarian crisis on an epic scale. Millions of families have been torn apart, pushed out of ancestral homes and forced to flee unspeakable horrors in search of safety and dignity. The emergence of ISIL, first in Syria and now holding territory in both Syria and Iraq, has exacerbated an already dire humanitarian crisis in Syria, where the Assad regime has waged a cruel and unrelenting campaign of bloodshed and starvation against its own people for almost four years.

There are now 10.8 million Syrian internally displaced persons (IDPs) and refugees— roughly half of Syria's pre-war population. That is almost equal to the combined populations of New York City and Chicago. With the crisis now engulfing Iraq, two million Iraqis have also been displaced since early 2014 due to ISIL attacks, with almost 200,000 new Iraqi refugees fleeing to neighboring countries, including Egypt, Iran, Jordan, Lebanon, Syria, Turkey, and the Gulf countries.

And, this crisis is radically rewriting the map of the region. Once the cradle of Nestorian Christianity, Mosul has been emptied of all Christians, ending a presence stretching back two millennia. Minority villages across Iraq and Syria have been ethnically cleansed. Reportedly about half a million Yezidis were slaughtered en masse, driven from ancestral homes in Ninewa and corralled on Mt. Sinjar, eventually seeking refuge in the Kurdistan region. ISIL summarily executed more than 200 Shia Turkmen and Shia Shabak in Tikrit and Mosul, forcing tens of thousands of families to flee. Sunnis throughout Iraq have also fled ISIL attacks, especially in Anbar. A massive outpouring of 3.2 million Syrians refugees throughout the region has transformed the demographics of neighboring countries, especially Lebanon where Syrians now make up more than a quarter of the population.

Women and children always bear the brunt of suffering in a conflict, but under ISIL, women and girls are suffering a special hell. ISIL has abducted, raped, and sold into sex slavery Yezidi and other minority women and girls—some as young as 12 years old. The United Nations Assistance Mission for Iraq (UNAMI) and the Office of the High Commissioner for Human Rights reports that ISIL is holding up to 2,500 Yezidi civilians, mostly women and children. In Kobani and elsewhere, young boys have been tortured and recruited as child soldiers, as documented by Human Rights Watch.

Today, I'd like to cover three key areas: First, an update on the U.S. government humanitarian response in Iraq and Syria, including our efforts to provide protection and assistance to the most vulnerable; second, how we are focusing on women and minorities to enable greater participation and hope for a better future; and finally, an outline of the key challenges that lie ahead as we seek to address these enormous needs with increasingly stretched resources.

The Humanitarian Situation

The humanitarian community is grappling with an unprecedented four Level 3 emergencies—the United Nation's (U.N.) most severe emergency designation. Syria and Iraq are two of these four emergencies, occurring against a global backdrop of rising crises that include Ukraine, South Sudan, Central African Republic, Nigeria— and now the Ebola epidemic in West Africa.

For the first time in USAID's history, our Office of U.S. Foreign Disaster Assistance has deployed four Disaster Assistance Response Teams (DARTs) and activated three Response Management Teams (RMTs) concurrently. The courageous work of USAID's humanitarian experts is saving lives around the globe in a tangible symbol of U.S. leadership and commitment to humanitarian action. At a time of unprecedented global need, however, we are also mounting aggressive efforts to mobilize international action. Increased commitments and collaboration from other donors are critical if we are to meet the escalating needs in Iraq and Syria.

Iraq and Syria are part of one overarching complex crisis with very fluid conflicts that shift borders and territory. However, the impact on people is markedly different. In Iraq, two million people are displaced in country, while a smaller number, 200,000, have fled to neighboring countries. Due to the rapid pace of displacement, most IDPs are living in camps, informal shelters or unfinished buildings, making shelter and heating an important concern for the winter. IDPs are now scattered across over 2,000 locations throughout the country, making centralized provision of humanitarian assistance difficult. Lack of access is also a major impediment. It is estimated that 2.2 million vulnerable Iraqis are located in ISIL-held areas in Al Anbar, Ninewa and Salah ad Din Governorates. Access issues in those areas make it impossible to know the level of humanitarian need.

The protracted nature of the Syrian conflict has resulted in humanitarian needs of a massive scale. There are 7.6 million IDPs in Syria, and another 3.2 million Syrians have fled to neighboring countries. The majority of those who are displaced inside Syria and in neighboring countries live in urban centers with extended family or friends that have offered them shelter, putting a massive strain on households and economies in major cities. Many of them have been uprooted more than once. The seemingly endless flow of Syrian refugees across borders has overwhelmed basic infrastructure in neighboring countries, including water, electricity, schools, and hospitals.

U.S. Humanitarian Response in Iraq

In early August, the world's attention focused on the plight of thousands of Yezidis, with mass killings reported in several parts of the Sinjar region. As this desperate scene unfolded and we received first-person accounts from individuals on Mt. Sinjar of the horrific conditions, we deployed one of our most seasoned DART leaders to coordinate with the U.S. military as they began an air drop operation to deliver crucial aid for thousands of trapped civilians. The U.S. military conducted seven nightly air drops between August 8-13, delivering more than 114,000 meals and 35,000 gallons of water to those displaced on Mt. Sinjar. The DART leader joined our Department of Defense (DoD) colleagues to conduct an on-the-ground assessment of the situation on Mt. Sinjar after the airdrops and concluded that the air drops reached thousands that otherwise likely would have perished. The opening of an eventual land route was critical in allowing Yezidis to move off of the mountain and away from the fighting and threat of ISIL. In Fiscal Year 2014, the U.S. government is providing more than $208 million in humanitarian assistance to meet the growing needs of those displaced by the spread of violence. Working through 12 UN and international NGO partners, we have delivered relief supplies; addressed emergency health needs; provided water, sanitation, and hygiene support; ensured emergency and transitional shelter; and addressed the massive protection and trauma needs of populations who have fled untold horrors.

ISIL has systematically targeted Yezidis, Shia, including members of the Shabak and Turkmen ethnic minority, and Sunnis who refuse to adhere to their extremist ideology. According to Human Rights Watch, ISIL has killed scores or even hundreds of male Yezidi civilians and carried off their relatives, forcing thousands of women into forced sexual servitude. In recent talks with Yezidi religious figures, they have shared with us a massive sense of fear and despair that their entire community will be wiped out from their ancestral lands. USAID remains committed to engaging closely with faith-based leaders, meeting regularly here in Washington and the region to hear and address concerns and ensure our aid continues to reach Yezidis and members of other minorities. Shia communities have also suffered relentless daily suicide and car bomb attacks against civilian centers, religious sites, open markets, and schools over the past 18 months, condemned by ISIL extremists as being "heretical" and "non-Muslim." The relentless targeting by ISIL aimed at removing religious and cultural diversity and denying freedom of belief is a horror to us all.

The Government of Iraq (GOI) and the Kurdish Regional Government (KRG) have also dedicated substantial funding, including a commitment of cash grants of $860 per displaced family that are being distributed by the Iraqi Ministry of Migration and Displacement. We are pleased to see this financial commitment and are working with Iraqi officials to ensure these resources are disbursed efficiently and without discrimination to all displaced communities, including Yezidis, Christians, and Shia Turkmen minorities. The KRG deserves special praise for offering refuge to more than 750,000 IDPs, along with over 220,000 refugees from Syria. A recent partner survey found that displaced communities are very satisfied and appreciative of the KRG's response. The Kingdom of Saudi Arabia's contribution of $500 million was essential as it scaled up the response at a critical time, including by supporting the World Food Program to distribute food aid to more than 1 million IDPs.

As winter ramps into full gear, we are working tirelessly with our partners to respond to potential cold-weather needs of over 150,000 members of the most vulnerable populations—including women, children, and religious and ethnic minorities. The State Department's Bureau of Population, Refugees, and Migration (PRM) has supported seven emergency airlifts by the U.N. High Commissioner for Refugees (UNHCR), delivering 25,000 tent insulation kits throughout Iraq. Clothing, kitchen sets, blankets, mattresses, and bedding, as well as materials to prepare shelter for winter conditions all provide dignity and a semblance of comfort in the midst of chaos. USAID has also begun to distribute cash grants of $100-$600 per family, especially in Dohuk where many Yezidis are displaced, offering greater freedom to IDPs to purchase seasonally appropriate items and much needed kerosene to help families endure the harsh winter.

Providing shelter with proper heating and sanitation facilities continues to be a priority for the winter. It is also critically important to clear schools that have been used for shelter, so that children can resume their education. In Dohuk Governorate, which is shouldering the largest number of IDPs, KRG officials have relocated 82,000 IDPs from schools to camps as of November 24, but another 450,000 IDPs remain in informal shelters or unknown locations. The KRG has made progress in evacuating virtually all schools, and we encourage the GOI and the KRG to continue constructing IDP camps that can be suitable shelter replacements with technical assistance from the UNHCR.

To assist with sanitation needs, USAID is helping to provide five liters of water per person per day in Dohuk and Ninewa Governorates while also supplying women and girls with hygiene supplies to stay healthy. A USAID partner is also strengthening the water and sanitation infrastructure in Diyala and Sulaymaniyah Governorates in concert with local authorities.

U.S. Humanitarian Response in Syria

While the pace of deterioration in Iraq is staggering, renewed focus on Iraq must be balanced with extraordinary needs in Syria. Violence from all sides in Syria has killed more than 200,000 people since March 2011, according to the Syrian Observatory for Human Rights, limited humanitarian access, and prompted widespread displacement. A UN report released on November 14 details the atrocities committed by ISIL in Syria, including forced displacement, kidnapping and disappearances, executions, amputations, public lashings and stoning, slavery and the recruitment of child soldiers. These abuses are layered on top of the Assad regime's indiscriminate killings and barrel bombings against their own people. Ongoing conflict has hindered the delivery of essential humanitarian assistance to populations in need, including in both regime and ISIL controlled areas of northern Syria.

In the midst of an ever more challenging security environment, the U.S. government continues to work through all possible channels— including more than 50 UN and international and Syrian NGOs—to meet the urgent humanitarian needs of more than 12.2 million people across all 14 governorates in Syria, and 3.2 million refugees in neighboring countries. Of the 12.2 million people in need throughout Syria, an estimated 4.8 million reside in UN-identified hard-to-reach areas, including 2.7 residing in areas of ISIL control. Despite access constraints throughout Syria, including in areas cut off by ISIL or regime forces, humanitarian actors are continuing to tirelessly work through all channels of assistance, including cross-border, cross line and operations from within Syria to access those in need throughout the country. In addition to significant ongoing NGO cross border operations, 558,000 people have benefitted from UN deliveries to northern Syria since the adoption of UN Security Council Resolution (UNSCR) 2165 in July, which authorizes the UN to cross border and conflict lines without approval by the regime.

The United States is the single largest donor in the Syrian crisis, and food aid is a big part of our assistance. The U.S. government is the largest contributor to the World Food Program (WFP)'s response to the Syrian crisis, providing $944 million since the crisis began. Through WFP, USAID delivers family rations and flour-to-bakeries programs reaching more than 4 million people inside Syria, and food vouchers, supplementary nutritional food and meal-replacement bars for 3.2 million refugees in neighboring countries. On November 22, Vice President Biden announced $135 million in new funding for ongoing emergency food needs in Syria and neighboring countries, primarily through assistance to WFP. Despite these latest contributions, WFP was forced to temporarily suspend its food aid to Syrian refugees in neighboring countries due to depleted funds. While new pledges and commitments this week will allow WFP to resume provision of food aid for Syrian refugees through December, the United States and its global partners will need to give more to meet the enormous demands for food aid and other humanitarian needs in the Syrian crisis. Funding from Congress is critical for USAID to provide additional support to WFP, and we look forward to Congressional approval of a full-year budget for Fiscal Year 2015, which will enable us to meet our humanitarian commitments for the new year.

USAID also continues to provide life-saving medical care during this brutal conflict. Nearly two million patients have been treated and more than 350,000 surgeries have been performed at 260 U.S. supported field hospitals, makeshift clinics, and medical facilities across the country. In October alone, USAID partners provided essential reproductive health care services, including emergency obstetric care, reproductive health vouchers and family planning activities for over 26,000 women in six governorates. We are also supporting mobile clinics to increase access to reproductive health services and clinical care for Gender Based Violence (GBV) victims in remote areas and IDP settlements. Recognizing the need for more medical staff capable of saving lives, we have trained more than 3,000 Syrian volunteers to provide emergency first-aid care, and actively recruit female health staff to meet the needs of female IDPs.

Through 18 partners, USAID is distributing winterization supplies—including warm clothing, blankets, mattresses, shoes, heating and fuel—and shelter support to help an estimated 1.5 million Syrians cope with the harsh weather and fend off health risks during the winter months.

Protecting Women and Children

Without a doubt women and children have been profoundly affected by these crises. Women have been the target of stoning, sex slavery, and other atrocities committed by ISIL. Recent reporting notes that 200,000 have died since the start of the conflict in Syria, with approximately 85 percent of the deceased being male. That figure alone is changing the sociological make-up of the country as women and young children are increasingly taking on roles that they had not previously filled. Almost half of the 12.2 million people in need of humanitarian assistance in the Syrian conflict are children, and 80 percent of three million Syrian refugees are women and children. Nearly three million Syrian children are out of school and growing increasingly vulnerable with each classroom destroyed. In Iraq, similar trends are occurring as displaced populations have taken up residence in schools. Behind these statistics is a generation of girls and boys yearning to shed the trauma of conflict and build a more prosperous and peaceful future.

Since 2012, USAID has been front and center in implementing the U.S. National Action Plan (NAP) on Women, Peace and Security, an essential roadmap for advancing gender equality and female empowerment, particularly of women and girls in crisis and conflict situations. As part of USAID's commitments within the Safe from the Start Initiative, and the US Government Action Plan on Children in Adversity, USAID has provided $26 million in humanitarian protection activities, including $10.5 million to respond to and reduce the risk of GBV and other abuses towards women in Syria and Iraq, as well as neighboring countries hosting refugees.

These programs have provided critical psychosocial support to help GBV survivors overcome the trauma of their past abuses and trained 360 psychosocial and healthcare workers to identify and respond to GBV cases in an appropriate way that does not stigmatize or further endanger survivors. One program in Idlib Governorate in Syria is providing a safe space for young displaced women to gather around workshops that provide information on hygiene and personal safety and skills-building sessions so that they are empowered to be self-reliant.

Another successful program is transforming attitudes around early marriages, which are on the rise among refugee communities. The Safety and Protection project waged an innovative media campaign that included 51 interactive plays, 270 lectures, TV and radio infomercials and social media messages that reached 9,000 individuals in remote and urban areas across Jordan to raise awareness about the dangers of early marriage, human trafficking, child labor and violence against women. The interactive plays evoked strong emotions from audience members who related to the stories that mirrored their lives.

USAID has also spent $15.4 million in child protection efforts that meet the objectives of No Lost Generation, an initiative by the international community that helps restore access to education and some sense of normalcy for Syrian children. USAID is providing learning and recreational opportunities for girls and boys that reduce the risk of exploitation, recruitment by armed groups, and abuse, and that help them develop life skills. USAID also supports case management and referral services for children at high risk of exploitation and abuse.

In central and southern Iraq, one USAID partner is deploying mobile protection teams that monitor and document human rights violation and abuses by state and non-state actors against displaced women and children. We have also built child-friendly spaces in displacement areas, such as in Erbil where 2,100 IDP children have received psychosocial support to improve their sense of safety and emotional well-being. USAID is also working in Diyala and Sulaymaniyah Governorates to establish family tracing and reunifications systems, as well as provide appropriate temporary care for separated and unaccompanied children and youth.

USAID partners also prioritize protection in all humanitarian efforts so that women and children have access to assistance that meets their needs. For instance, USAID partners in Syria and Iraq are ensuring that relief kits contain women and infant hygiene supplies; installing separate toilets and showers for women and with inside locks to increase safety; and building latrines near tents.

Promoting Inclusion and Empowerment of Women and Minorities

Iraq

For over a decade, USAID has laid groundwork for locally-owned governance and rule of law in Iraq, and at a local level we have seen results, including greater empowerment of women and minorities. Our ongoing Access to Justice (A2J) Program, which established a legal assistance network of 25 civil society and law school clinics across 13 governorates, has helped 18,000 Iraqis file for identity documents and seek legal protections. Three-quarters of these have been women, including many who needed to register their marriages so that they could receive benefits to which they are entitled under Iraqi law.

When entire communities were displaced by ISIL, they often left behind or destroyed identity documents as they fled out of fear of retribution if identified as a non-Sunni Muslim or part of a minority group. In response, the A2J program pivoted to work with IDPs and the GOI to help those who fled replace identification documents essential to government and international assistance, greatly easing the burdens of Christians and other minority groups who had fled and restoring their sense of identity and security.

Further, USAID's "Foras" (Arabic for "Opportunities") project has secured over 9,300 job placements for job-seekers, 25 percent women, through its online jobs portal and partner agencies, and trained more than 20,000 Iraqis in job-related skills. In the wake of the crisis, this program has provided short-term labor opportunities for IDPs—because we know that a job is preferred to humanitarian aid in both the short- and long-term.

Syria

In Syria, we are empowering Syrian women leaders to play a more active role in transition planning and peace negotiations, in keeping with UNSCR 1325 and our objectives under the NAP for Women, Peace, and Security. We believe that support for Syrian women bolsters opposition credibility, increases pressure for a negotiated settlement, and effectively counters extremists. We have trained more than 500 Syrian women so that they are equipped with essential advocacy and negotiation skills to contribute to high-level and community-level peacebuilding efforts. We also provided support to help an impressive group of women leaders create the Syrian Women's Network. I have met these women many times over the last three years, witnessing firsthand their transformation into powerful change agents and peace brokers. We supported the women from the network so that they could participate in the Geneva II negotiations, where they shared compelling messages about the devastating impact of the conflict and the need for peace. We also trained several women who ran in provisional local council elections in liberated areas of Aleppo last December.

These advances are nevertheless constrained within the greater context of a shrinking space for civil society and nascent local governance structures inside Syria, due to the violence perpetrated by the Syrian regime, ISIL and other terrorist groups' exploitation of ungoverned spaces. But I am confident that these simple acts of female empowerment are critical for Syria's future.

Key Challenges Ahead

The crises in Iraq and Syria are stretching the international humanitarian community to the brink of capacity, underscoring the need for increased commitments and coordination among foreign donors. The GOI and the KRG must also continue to address the pressing needs of their citizens. Given the fluid security situation, it is difficult to predict where humanitarian needs will unfold, particularly in light of broader political and security concerns.

Humanitarian access will also remain the central challenge, particularly in ISIL-held and contested areas where attempts at negotiated access have fallen short. The U.S. government and our Syria and Iraq DART teams will continue to work with the humanitarian community – including the UN and international and national non-governmental organizations, U.S. military, and other partners on the ground to ensure a rapid and agile response to shifting humanitarian needs, especially as needs are more clearly identified in southern Iraq.

As sectarian violence roils much of Iraq, displaced persons may be unable or unwilling to return home, and atrocity prevention efforts will be ever more important. We anticipate enormous needs in liberated areas to help communities recover, prevent cycles of retaliatory violence and atrocities, and fill critical governance gaps.

On October 23, the U.N. released a revised Strategic Response Plan for Iraq, laying out a longer-term strategy, which estimates that $2.2 billion will be needed to address ongoing humanitarian needs through 2015. USAID is working closely with our U.N. colleagues to determine how we can most appropriately leverage our resources to support another long-term response. The Kingdom of Saudi Arabia's historic contribution of $500 million in humanitarian relief funds, as well as support from Turkey, Oman, Bahrain, Kuwait, Brunei Darussalam, Qatar and the United Arab Emirates has been critical, but more partners will need to step up to meet these growing needs.

In Syria, the needs inside the country continue to mount with ISIL's offensives and the Assad regime's continuing campaigns in Syrian cities. Concerted attention and assistance is needed to help relieve the strain on host countries, especially Lebanon where Syrians now make up more than 25 percent of the population. Despite an enormous response and commitment by the U.S. government and other donors, we struggle to keep pace with ever growing needs almost four years into the crisis. On December 18, the U.N. will release its Strategic Response Plan for Syria, which will inevitably require greater commitments from all donors. USAID will continue to work with other donors, the U.N. and partners to leverage and pool all resources to try to meet these demands.

Conclusion

Forging strong partnerships will be critical to meet the immense challenges and needs ahead in Iraq and Syria. As part of our commitment to ending extreme poverty and promoting resilient, democratic societies, USAID will continue to provide life-saving, needs-based assistance and protect and empower women and minorities, while pushing to secure access to additional populations currently trapped in areas controlled by ISIL.

Our hearts are with the thousands of people who remain trapped in unsustainable situations, and we are gravely concerned for the health and safety of these displaced men, women, and children, besieged by acts of violence committed by ISIL, the Syrian regime, and other extremists.

USAID is deeply appreciative of Congressional support to provide the resources that makes our humanitarian work possible in Syria and Iraq.

Testimony of Sarah Margon

Washington Director, Human Rights Watch

Senate Foreign Relations Committee

Subcommittee on International Operations and Organizations,

Human Rights,

Democracy and Global Women's Issues

December 9, 2014

"ISIL's Reign of Terror: Confronting the Growing Humanitarian

Crisis in Iraq and Syria"

Madam Chair, members of the Committee, thank you for inviting me to testify this morning. It is a great pleasure to be here. Per your request, I would like to share some insights from my recent trip to Iraq and then touch on Syria, where the Islamic State in Iraq and al-Sham, or ISIS, is one of many groups, including the Syrian government, perpetrating gross and widespread violations of international human rights and humanitarian law.

Human Rights Watch has been documenting ISIS-related abuses in Syria and Iraq since August 2013. While we have not traveled to ISIS-held territory because of security concerns, we have conducted extensive interviews with those that have fled the armed group as well as with many people who are still living in areas under their control. Until recently, we made numerous trips to northern Syria. We still travel regularly to interview Syrians and Iraqis in Jordan, Turkey, and Lebanon in addition to many parts of Iraq, where I spent a week in early October.

By now, ISIS' extraordinary brutality is well known. Their campaign of killings is remarkably gruesome — they hide nothing, promote their atrocities via social media, and make clear they don't subscribe to the same norms, values, laws, and standards that serve to guide the international community. Instead, ISIS employs an overt strategy of cruelty to sow fear and subdue populations under its control, bolstered by tactics that seem to be a throwback, if you will, to another era.

But ISIS didn't come from nowhere. In fact, they have been gaining strength for quite some time — taking advantage of the brutal crackdown by Syrian and Iraqi authorities, the marginalization of Sunnis that began over a decade ago after the US invasion of Iraq, and the conflict-related chaos in Syria, to name but a few. Similarly, the rapid territorial gains ISIS made this summer were largely enabled by the discontent that resulted from the Maliki-led government policies that fed a cycle of sectarian violence through exclusion and discrimination.

Iraq

In early October, I traveled about two hours south of Kirkuk to learn more about the role of Shia militias in the ground fight against ISIS. My colleague and I had heard numerous anecdotes about the ransacking of Sunni villages by government-backed militias after the US-coalition airstrikes helped "liberate" Amerli, a predominately Shia town of approximately 12,000 people under ISIS siege for almost two months. While they did play a role liberating that village, what we learned that day confirmed a devastating picture of relentless arson, destruction, displacement, and killings committed by various militias, with impunity. At the end of our visit, we pulled off the highway to speak with a family displaced by the recent violence. A man in his late 40s, who was living in an abandoned strip mall, told me, "I am no more afraid of Daesh" — the Arabic acronym for the Islamic State — "than I am of the Shia militias and the Iraqi government."

The circumstances around the post-Amerli siege are emblematic of a larger and deeply worrisome effort underway throughout much of Iraq as it scales up its counterterrorism campaign with support from the United States: crudely empowered Shia militias are being used to punish the Sunni population because of its sect.

In the weeks that followed my visit, our team went to more than 20 predominately Sunni villages and heard consistent accounts of systematic destruction by Shia militias that are determined to prevent villagers from returning. Hundreds of families were left homeless, searching for shelter in abandoned factories, graveyards, and under cars and trucks. This tactic intensifies sectarian tensions throughout the country and appears to be flourishing in the absence of any larger strategy for civilian protection.

Meanwhile, ISIS preys on vulnerable communities, including those historically concentrated in the Nineveh plains, such as the Chaldo-Assyrian Christians, Shia Shabaks, Turkmen, and Yezidis. These groups have a long history of marginalization but ISIS has intensified this ostracism, labeling them as crusaders, heretics, and devil-worshipers and then threatening them with death if they don't convert to Islam.

Six weeks ago, I traveled not far from the Syrian border to Dohuk to interview young Yezidi men, women and girls who had recently escaped ISIS captivity. They described harrowing tales of cramped detention, abuse, forced conversion, forced marriage, and sexual slavery. One 15-year-old girl we interviewed—who had only arrived back with her family the day before—was taken from Mosul to Raqqa, Syria. Along the way, she was detained in four different locations, including in Badoush prison, near Mosul, with hundreds of other Yezidis. While there, she said she saw fighters take more than 100 boys, some as young as six years old, from their mothers. Maybe they were sent to be "reeducated" or maybe to a training camp. It is likely they were all forced to convert; maybe some were killed.

When this girl arrived in Raqqa after her grueling journey, she said she was detained in a private home with about 20 other girls, only to be sold a few days later to an ISIS fighter for about $1000.

Another Yezidi girl we interviewed was held captive with her four sisters, the youngest of whom was 10 years old. She shared the story of another young girl, with whom she was detained and who had been "selected" by an older ISIS fighter. He regularly took her to his home, locked her in a room and told his family he was "helping her with her Islamic education." Instead, he was beating and raping her.

Our team has also documented ISIS efforts to recruit children as fighters, to encourage them to volunteer for suicide attacks and to force them to learn Sharia (Islamic law) and jihadist ideology.

Madam Chair, as you will recall this past August, President Obama made clear the United States would "not turn a blind eye"[1] to a Yezidi massacre in Iraq. Certainly, there has been increased attention to the plight of the Yezidis, alongside other vulnerable communities in Iraq, but launching a military operation isn't a sufficient long-term strategy to protect these groups – or any others.

Indeed, thousands of families have already been torn apart; more than 500,000 Yezidis and other religious minorities have been driven from their homes, most to the semi-autonomous region of Kurdistan, which is already suffering under the strain of some 200,000 Syrian refugees and lacks the resources to mount an adequate response.[2]

---

[1] White House, "Statement by the President," August 7, 2014, http://www.whitehouse.gov/the-pressoffice/ 2014/08/07/statement-president (accessed December 8, 2014).

[2] UNHCR, "Syria Regional Refugee Response," 2014, http://data.unhcr.org/syrianrefugees/country.php?id=103 (accessed December 8, 2014).

But it is not only religious minorities who have been displaced. Thousands of Sunni families are also fleeing violence in other parts of Iraq, including in areas recently "cleared" of ISIS that are less accessible and virtually invisible to the international community. Countrywide, there are now more than 1.8 million displaced Iraqis, many of whom have little access to basic services or any meaningful protection.

Syria

In Syria, where ISIS has been able to use the chaos of armed conflict to consolidate its powerbase and grow its membership, communities have been reeling from widespread human rights violations by all sides. In fact, the main threat to many civilians does not come from ISIS but from the Syrian government—which continues to brutally target its own population with barrel bombs and other conventional weapons. Healthcare and education systems in rebel-held parts of the country have broken down while nine million people have been driven from their homes. Neighboring countries are swollen with refugees and regional stability is increasingly under threat.

Within this context, US-led airstrikes to counter ISIS are acutely juxtaposed against the absence of any real plan for civilian protection throughout the country, particularly in ISIS-held territory. Here, the issue is not just whether individual strikes have hit—or targeted—civilians but also what the cumulative effect will be for Syrians who remain in ISIS-controlled areas, under brutal conditions.

Already, residents of Raqqa are reporting an increase in the price of basic commodities, particularly fuel needed for heating, as a result of the strikes on ISIS refineries. Within days of the first airstrikes in Syria, major protests raised concerns not only about the myopic focus of the US-led campaign but also about the potential for any related civilian deaths to increase ISIS recruitment.

The administration should take this concern very seriously. Just like in Iraq, all the horrors caused by ISIS—or any of the other armed groups aligned with them—are not going to be eliminated by airstrikes. In fact, without a larger conversation about genuine protection measures for Syrians at risk there is a real possibility they could make the situation significantly worse.

Recommendations

The growing crises in Iraq and Syria are distinct but increasingly interlinked. They will require sustained engagement from concerned governments, and the United States in particular, for many years to come. That said, there are some near-term steps Human Rights Watch would like to suggest that could provide a measure of protection and support for those in need.

First, as the administration should publicly commit to investigate airstrikes in both Iraq and Syria in which civilians were casualties in possible violation of the laws of armed conflict, publicly report on the findings, and commit to appropriate redress in cases of wrongdoing. The administration should also consider providing assistance to any civilians harmed in US airstrikes, as was done in Afghanistan. Congress should press the administration to do this and ensure they have appropriate resources.

Second, in both Iraq and Syria, the US needs to take great care as it scales up its engagement with state security forces and armed groups. Comprehensive vetting mechanisms need to be in place to ensure the US is not supporting abusive groups or commanders—or that US taxpayer dollars are lost to graft. In general, human rights vetting for security forces needs to be robust, consistent, and incorporated into a wider plan for reform that seeks to build an integrated force with civilian protection at the center of its mandate.

In Syria, the administration has committed to developing such a program for the moderate rebels and, while Human Rights Watch doesn't take a position on it, we do believe vetting is an essential part of making sure training and weapons do not end up in the wrong hands. It is too early to tell if the initiative will be successful but Congress can play an active role making sure it is consistently applied and regularly monitored.

In Iraq, certain security force units well known for their abusive tactics should be omitted from the reform process until the government takes steps towards remediation. Congress should also press the administration to develop clear policy guidance on how diplomats and military officials can support the Iraqis and other foreign governments to promote accountability. As you may know, the Leahy Law requires the administration to offer related assistance but this area of the law and associated policy are woefully underdeveloped. Finally, on this point, strong congressional oversight will be essential to ensure Baghdad does not funnel US government-issued weapons and equipment to Shia militias or into their own pockets, which appears to be happening already with some regularity.

Third, and specifically with regard to Iraq, there is the need for the US to scale-up support for nonmilitary initiatives throughout the country, whether independent activists, media, relief aid, or civil society organizations. Such support is an important counter balance to military operations and helps promote a culture of oversight and public accountability – both of which are sorely missing.

In northern Iraq, this assistance should include support for local and international organizations to increase medical and counseling services for displaced people who fled ISIS. Programs should be geared towards the confidential needs of people who have survived sexual violence, including comprehensive post-rape care. Access to Iraqis outside Kurdistan—and information about the conditions in which they're living—remains extremely limited. Scaled-up support to impartial groups, including in the Anbar region, should be a priority and would indicate a commitment to all Iraqis.

Finally, when it comes to Syria it is clear that the underlying problem continues to be one of largescale insecurity. No amount of humanitarian aid can suffice for the absence of greater protection. Nonetheless, the US should redouble its efforts to see UN Security Council Resolution 2139 implemented in a meaningful way. This means leading the Security Council to press for an end to indiscriminate attacks on civilians in Syria— including the government's use of barrel bombs, calling on all sides to release civilian detainees – including the thousands of people held by the Syrian government in inhumane conditions, and ensuring relief aid consistently reaches those in need.

Madam Chair, the grim reality is that ISIS is going to be around for the foreseeable future, as are the conditions that have enabled it to thrive. So instead of thinking predominately about military operations against ISIS, there is a need to shift gears and reflect on how the US can do a better job helping civilians find a greater measure of protection while also ensuring US military operations do not inadvertently end up strengthening ISIS appeal to disenfranchised Sunnis. If the US doesn't take this step, far too many people in Iraq and Syria will continue living in brutal conditions, under constant threat from a wide range of abusive actors, and without sufficient support for their most basic human needs.

Testimony of Vian Dakhil, Yezidi Minister of Parliament, in the Iraqi central government before the
Senate Foreign Relations Subcommittee on International Operations and Organizations, Human Rights, Democracy, and Global Women's Issues
Hearing entitled "ISIL's Reign of Terror: Confronting the Growing Humanitarian Crisis in Iraq and Syria"
December 9, 2014

Dear members of the Senate, ladies and gentleman …. Good Morning.

Chairwoman Boxer, ranking member Senator Rand Paul, and members of the subcommittee:

I would like to begin by thanking you and thanking your staff for convening this hearing and giving me an opportunity to speak today about the horrors experienced by my people... the Yezidis of the Kurdish Region. I thank you for your leadership and for your compassion, and ask that you hear our plea for help to meet the most critical crisis facing our people in our long and painful history.

My name is Vian Dakhil. I am the only Yezidi Minister of Parliament in the Iraqi central government and a member of the Kurdistan Democratic Party. I was born in Mosul in 1973. My father's work as a doctor moved our family to various towns and villages before finally settling in Erbil, the capital of the Kurdish Region in 1984.

Since the invasion of the "so called Islamic State" (IS) in June 2014, I have been working tirelessly to bring attention to the plight of the Yezidi people and the acts of genocide committed against them by the IS.

Let me begin by saying the Yezidi people have suffered many acts of genocide over the course of our history. Many thousands have been persecuted and killed because of our beliefs. The number of surviving Yezidis in northern Iraq, southern Turkey, and eastern Syria now does not exceed 600,000, and many are living in refugee camps with minimal support.

I traveled myself to Mt. Sinjar to deliver emergency aid to the Yezidis fleeing IS. Our helicopter crashed resulting in the death of several on board. I suffered injuries, but was fortunate to continue the struggle to help those in need.

The stories told by refugees are heartbreaking. A woman recently called me at 2 am in the morning to recount that she had fled her village with her five children after IS slaughtered her husband. Two of the children died of thirst; one was left disabled on the mountain because she had to keep running to save the lives of her remaining two children. Imagine yourself having to choose which one of your children will live? This is only one example of thousands ... Yezidis who have witnessed family members massacred, who fled chaotically not knowing whether they will live to see tomorrow. They fled with no family, no shelter, no food and no water.

Our women and girls have been targeted by IS and kidnapped and raped. No doubt you have heard the many stories of indescribable suffering by these poor women, treated as sexual slaves and sold and traded as property. This continues with many Yezidi women still being held and suffering at the hands of IS. It believed that at least 3,000 Yezidis are still in captivity IS hands in Iraq and Syria.

There are 700 hundred families still trying to survive on Mt. Sinjar. They do not have enough shelter, food or medical to survive the winter.

Many Yezidis have fled the IS controlled areas and are living in refugee camps in the region. The cities of Zakho and Dohuk in Iraqi Kurdistan have tried to accommodate some of these refugees. Two thirds of all schools in those two cities have been converted to temporary housing for Yezidis and other refugees fleeing IS. Others are living in make shift tent cities that are exposed to the harsh winter weather. Supplies, humanitarian aid, and medical assistance are far from adequate for these people.

We come here today to ask for your help. The Christians in Iraq and elsewhere have a powerful lobby. They have the strong support of the European nations and the Vatican. Many are being offered political asylum. We, the Yezidis, are a small minority. We do not have advocates. I ask for your compassion and support.

We ask you for immediate support to get the Yezidis through this difficult winter. We ask for your help for a long term solution that protects the Yezidi people from further persecution.

We have lived in the region for thousands of years preserving our heritage, our religion and our land. We feel that IS is determined to exterminate the Yezidi people. After the recent massacres, and the inhumane torture of our women, we are desperate to protect what is left of our people and our religion. If it means leaving the land to protect our people, we are willing to do so to protect our identity and future generations.

We are here to plead for your help … to support the refugees survive the dire short term challenges of this winter. And we ask you to support the Yezidi people in finding a long term solution that protects Yezidis from annihilation. The world cannot allow another genocide to occur.

Thank you for giving me an opportunity to appear before this subcommittee.

Testimony of Bishop Francis Kalabat from the St. Thomas the Apostle Chaldean Catholic Diocese
Senate Subcommittee on International Operations and Organizations, Democracy and Global Women's Issues
December 9, 2014

Madam Chair, Ranking Member, members of the committee: My name is Francis Kalabat and I serve as Bishop of the Chaldean Diocese of St. Thomas in North America, which includes 12 churches in Michigan and Illinois representing more than 175,000 Chaldean Catholics in communion with Rome and His Holiness Pope Francis.

Thank you for allowing me to testify before you today. As I speak, the process of the eradication of Christians in Iraq and throughout the Middle East continues. Ten years ago, in Iraq alone, there were over 350 Churches; today there are fewer than forty. Many have been bombed or destroyed; others, especially in the historically Christian villages of northern Iraq, are being used as Islamic State facilities.

I am here today to give testimony to the suffering of our people in Iraq and throughout the diaspora in Jordan, Lebanon, Syria and Turkey, and to seek further assistance from this body, Congress as a whole and the executive branch. The United States has a unique role and obligation in this conflict. Not only because we are the standard bearer and protector of international human rights, but also because the plight of Christians in Iraq today is a direct result of the U.S.-led invasion of Iraq in 2003.

That effort, the poorly planned and executed goal of regime change and the more recent withdrawal of U.S. troops, left in its wake a weakened and decentralized national government, sectarian warfare and the practice of government by tribes or in some cases government by gang. The lack of national unity and a tepid Iraqi military has left a dangerous void—a void filled, hopefully only temporarily, by Islamic State—a group that is the anathema to the West, to Judeo-Christian values and to civilized international norms. This has meant devastating consequences to the people of Iraq, especially Christians who are being systematically uprooted from their homes in the historical birthplace of Christianity.

A couple hundred thousand Christian Iraqis have fled their homes since the militant Islamic State group swept through much of the north in June. Islamic State has been turning churches into prisons in the Iraq city of Mosul, which used to be the site of a large Christian community before it was driven out by this terrorist group. As an example, Fides News Agency reported last Tuesday that a number of detainees were recently sent to the ancient Chaldean church of the Immaculate Conception in the eastern part of the city. Sources have shared that the historically important St. George Monastery in the north has also been turned into a place for female detention, raising fears that women might be abused. Our Churches have been destroyed and many of our ancient manuscripts dating back to the tenth century have been destroyed in an effort to wipe out our identity.

Mosul has been emptied of Christians who, under the implementation of Sharia law, have been forced to convert to Islam, pay a tax, leave their homes or die for their faith. Many have been killed in the name of religion.

Allow me to quote from a letter from Sr. Maria Hanna, Prioress of the Dominican Sisters of St. Catherine of Siena in Iraq.

"After four months of exile there are no signs of hope that the situation here in Iraq will be resolved peacefully. Unable to think or make decisions, everything is vague and we feel as if we have been living a nightmare. Christianity in Iraq is bleeding; so many families have left, and many are leaving to Lebanon, Jordan, and Turkey, preparing themselves for second immigration and an uncertain future. We know not how long these families will be able to tolerate the burden and survive financially.

"The conditions remain the same for those of us in Iraq. Many still are forced to stay in unfinished buildings on construction sites. In one place, a mall has been remodeled to accommodate families, with the hall divided merely with partitions. Although they are better than tents, they resemble dark, damp cages with no ventilation. Most difficult of all is the lack of privacy.

"There have been some attempts to provide containers and rent houses and flats, but this is not enough as the number of displaced people increases each day. Many come from cold mountainous places. Psychologically, people are tired, worried, confused, and irritated – who would blame them? They are jobless, their children do not attend school, and young people are still waiting to start their academic year at the university – some tried to register at Kurdish universities, but they were not accepted. All this is causing tremendous strain on the families, and the result is abuse and relationships that are unhealthy. The problems are totally overwhelming, and it seems as if our efforts are amounting to nothing.

"People have been stripped of their dignity…." End quote.

Members of this Committee, I submit to you that when people lose their dignity, they despair and despair is a dark, lonely place. But as our Savior Jesus Christ has taught us, "Where there is despair, he will bring hope." But it is incumbent on us—the United States, western nations and all God-loving people everywhere, to be the tools and the manifestation of this hope. Therefore, I call on this sub-committee and the United States government to resolve the following:

1) Our Diocese here has raised more than $1.5 million to aid the internally displaced Christians and other minorities now living in Kurdistan. Banking laws and regulations and other stipulations should not inhibit this money from reaching the people who need it.

2) The Kurdish government should be provided resources by the U.S. specifically to aid people displaced by this current conflagration. The Kurdish Regional Government lacks resources to aid our growing refugee community and the arms to combat these terrorists.

3) Pressure should be placed on the central government in Baghdad to take a more active stance on the growing problem of Iraqi refugees. The central government has done virtually nothing to support our community and is primarily concerned with the preservation of sectarian political power. Christians are being used as pawns because we have lived in what is known as disputed areas in Iraq.

4) The U.S. and the international community must immediately intervene to provide direct humanitarian aid to the displaced Christians and other minorities in the regions of Erbil and Dohuk in northern Iraq.

5) Christian and other minority villages that have been overrun by ragtag Islamic State militants must immediately be liberated with U.S. military assistance and refugees provided safe passage to return to their villages and homes.

6) The Christian and other minority villages must be protected by a U.S.-led international force under the supervision of either the U.S. or United Nations, if other governments will participate. The air strikes alone are accomplishing very little and costing taxpayers a bundle.

7) Syria must not follow the same path as Iraq. The United States' involvement in Syria is just as vague as that in Iraq and is leading to the same brutality. This only leads us to ask: Who's next in the Middle East?

Senators, I submit to you that the U.S. must finish what it started; Islamic State must be defeated quickly and permanently. They are a menace to the Iraqi and Syrian people and will be a permanent threat to the West if they are not dismantled. The situation that the ancient Christian people of Iraq find themselves in today is the direct result of 20 years of failed U.S. policy in Iraq. An additional 2.2 million Christians in Syria are facing the same fate. Our response and future actions as a government cannot be borne just from a sense of humanitarian responsibility but rather the moral obligation that accompanies the direct role that the U.S has played in the destabilization of Iraq and the region.

www.ingramcontent.com/pod-product-compliance
Lightning Source LLC
Chambersburg PA
CBHW081117280526
45787CB00007B/2864